TRAINING DISCIPLES ACA

This Manual is designed to give the student successful methodologies of Christian teaching. This course is also designed to help the student develop skills to understand and apply the scriptures to their personal lives. In addition, it is the basis for ongoing training and development. Develop the ability of each student to apply the Scriptures to life situations.

This book is designed to help Pastors equip their leaders with some of the knowledge, wisdom, character and skills needed to serve within a local church that explores the attitudes, thinking and application of the ministry. It is based on the Scriptures and experience, in that order.

This is expected to allow pastors and leaders and small group students to better manage their meetings and those involved. It is also expected to help pastors train church planters and launch teams to support church planters. In addition to these goals, it is ultimately expected to assist in the development of students, and leaders to help the Pastor to Pastor by preaching, visiting and showing care.

"Take the teachings that you heard me proclaim in the presence of many witnesses, and entrust them to reliable people, who will be able to teach others also."

Second Timothy 2: 2

YOUR HEART

Session 1 The need

Session 2 The requirements

Session 3 Your ministry

Session 4 Character in development

Session 5 Divine Motivation

1. The heart

• God has taken care to continue

• Attitudes have been sanctified (Philippians 2: 5)

• Relationship problems have been resolved (Matthew 5: 23-24)

• We are open enough for God to accept his correction (Hebrews 12: 1-4)

• We are open to experience God (Acts 1: 8)

In most of the groups (political party, religious, society, sports club, etc.) there is a leader, who is characterized by occupying the highest position within the group.

The essence of leadership

What is a leader?

1. An example / pattern for others

2. One able to chart the course for others to follow

3. One disciplined enough to be responsible for a group of others

4. First participant of what is suggested as a possibility

5. One who takes responsibility for himself and others for productivity

6. One who is responsible for the transition of people.

What is legitimately expected from a leader?

* Integrity: unites the hearts of people with a leader

* Consistency: teaches people to value collective effort [process]

* Initiative: kill the spirit of complacency in an atmosphere

* Discipline: makes your leadership credible [Notice that perfection is not in the list above]

What is it that usually undermines dynamic leadership?

Critical spirits / wrong approaches

Unverified character problem

Lack of connection with people

Failure to serve the needs of people

Impure motives

Lack of adjustment / change when ordered by God

Never anything from the outside

Leadership examples:

1-Do not participate in what you do not understand [know the person and the vision of the person with whom he works]

2-Never give advice before applying it to yourself first

3- Before participating, know where we have been, where we are, where we are going [remember that you are now "us"]

4-Assume the role of the server and the student, no matter what's their EXPERIENCE

5. Strive to be an agent of Progress or automatically become part of the obstacle.

6. Place your gifts at the leaders' feet, without expecting anything in return

7. Be devout and demanding as to how to commit without interrupting

8. Do not compare ministries, live and serve in the present.

Time to be DISCIPLES

Making disciples: Known as the Great Commission Matthew 28:19 "Go, therefore, and teach all the nations, baptizing them in the name of the Father, and of the Son, and of the Holy Spirit, teaching them to observe all that I have commanded you. and behold, I am with you always, until the end of the age. "

"The process"

Selection of the 12 disciples

Luke 6: 12-13

Disciple: a follower or student

"The process" Stages of development

the Convert

the disciple

the worker

leader

"The process"

Temporary Mark for Development

Convert to discipleship 2 years

Disciple of workers-2 years

Leadership worker 3 years

Ex: Jesus spent 3.5 years.

"The Process" 2 Timothy 2: 2

Commit: Suggest to transmit something from one person to another (this takes time)

Faithful: Elijah / teach Elisha: you cannot teach effectively what you do not live and know

Selection criteria for Disciples' Perspective

It has been adopted as its objective, the same objective God establishes in His Word. He is willing to pay any price to see the will of God fulfilled in his life. He has a love for the Word of God. He has a servant's heart He puts no trust in the flesh He does not have an independent spirit He has a love for people He does not let himself be trapped by bitterness He has learned to discipline his Disciples of life They are Made not Born; He must have a vision of impact in the world and make disciples

Disciplines of a Disciple

*Memorization of scriptures daily.

*Daily reading of the Bible and diligent study.

* Daily worship, prayer and meditation.

*Daily application of Scripture in the life of the disciple. People do what they do not what they say

* weekly fast

*Daily quiet time

*Weekly time of accountability

Role of the Disciple

To fulfill the Great Commission: go make disciples, baptize, teach

This means that the Great Commission is not only to go to the ends of the earth preaching the Gospel, or to baptize a large number of converts in the name of God but, teach them the precepts of Christ to make disciple to build people, such as those who were so limited by the Commission of Christ that they not only followed their way, but made others as well. Only disciples could the other activities of the commission fulfill their purpose.

Pop quiz

What is the Great Commission?

What is a disciple?

What are some of the qualities of a disciple?

What are some of the daily disciplines of a disciple?

What should a disciple do?

Name some of the costs of discipleship?

Memory Verses 2 Corinthians 5:17 Galatians 2:20

Feedback

What are some of your expectations?

How long have you been a Christian?

Are you willing to commit to your growth?

Leadership with vision

Strategic planning

Visionary leadership

Leaders with strong visionary leadership had the highest performing teams

Weak leaders in vision and management skills had low performance teams.

Why the need for visionary leadership? Provides guidance for daily decisions: keeps everyone pointing in the same direction

Act as your magnetic north leadership is about going somewhere. If you and your people do not know where you are going, your leadership does not matter. "

4 factors that affect all Teams

Overview

1. Define leadership

2. Define leadership styles

3. Define the Leadership Traits

4. Define bases of leadership power

Definition of leader

Write the first 5 names you think of when someone says leader.

The position or function of a leader

The action of directing a group of people or an organization

Influence: the ability or power of people or things to be a convincing force or produce effects on actions, behaviors, opinions, etc. of others. The action of producing effects on actions, behavior, opinions, etc. of others

Authoritarian leaders' Authoritarian leaders exert influence and control over group members

Praise / criticism is freely given, but is based on personal standards.

Results of the authoritarian style

Positive results:

Efficient and productive

Negative Results:

It can create hostility and discontent

Democratic style

The leader does not speak to the members of the group; rather, they speak to those they feel are at the same level

Democrat style results

Positive results:

Greater satisfaction, commitment and cohesion of group members

Negative Results:

It can cause inefficiencies and lower productivity

Lazy style

Typically considered non-leader

Positive results:

None

Negative Results:

The members of the group are discouraged

Server constructs empathy, integrity, self-awareness, influence, vision, development of others

Direct, trainer, supportive, delegate, listens, openness, warmth

Transactional Targeted task, negotiable, reward in exchange for the desired behavior

Transformational Charisma, care, agents of change, influence, respect, loyalty, inspiration, visionary, build a solid relationship with followers.

6 Most valuable leadership traits

* Intelligence

* Trust

* Charisma

* Determination

* Sociability

* Integrity

Bases of leadership power

Coercive Force: Instills fear, such as punishment, unwanted work assignments, reprimands or dismissals.

Power of connection: Power derives from connections made with influential and important people.

Expert power: Power which is demonstrated through experience, skill and knowledge to influence the work behaviors of others.

Power of information: Maintains influence because others need or want information and knowledge, which is an added value.

Theology: The study of God

Theology

- Theos: God

- Ology: The Study of

God's Attributes the Greatness of God

The Names of God/Attributes

Omnipotent - all powerful

Omnipresent- everywhere at the same time

Omniscient-knows everything

The greatness of God

The immanence of God; - Jeremiah 23:24

The transcendence of God - Isaiah 55: 8-9

More attributes:

God is love God is just

• The immutability of God

Revelations of the Old Testament

Jireh: The Lord will provide Genesis 22: 13-14

Sabboath: The Lord of hosts Isaiah 6: 1-3

Nissi: The Lord is my banner Exodus 17:15

Rohi: The Lord my shepherd Psalm 23: 1

Shalom: The Lord is Peace Judges 6:24

Rapha: The Lord our Healer Exodus 15:26

Sama: The Lord is here Ezekiel 48:35

Mekkadesh: The Lord your Sanctifier Exodus 31:13

Names of the old testament

"EL" means God

El-Elyon – the highest God Genesis 14: 17-20

El-Shaddai - all sufficient Genesis 17: 1, Psalm 91: 1

El-Roi - the God who sees me Genesis 16:13

Elohim - God II Corinthians 9:17

Hashem - The name Leviticus 24:11, 16, Deuteronomy 28:50

Pneumatology "The Study of the Holy Spirit"

Romans 12: 6-8

- Prophecy

- Service

- Teaching

- Exhortation

- Liberality

- Donation Aid

- Acts of Mercy

The gifts of the Spirit

- 1. Word of Wisdom

- 2. Word of Knowledge

- 3. Faith

- 4. The gifts of healing

- 5. Work of Miracles

- 6. Prophecy

- 7. discernment of spirits

- 8. Various tongues

- 9. Interpretation of Tongues - 1 Corinthians 12: 8-10

3 Divisions

1. Revelation

2. Power

3. Vocal

Revelatory

1. Word of Knowledge

2. Word of Wisdom

3. discernment of spirits

Word of Knowledge

The special ability to discover, accumulate, analyze and clarify information
and ideas that are relevant to the well-being of the body of Christ.

Word of wisdom

The ability to understand the mind of the Holy Spirit in such a way as to receive
an idea of how knowledge can be applied to the specific needs that arise in the body of Christ.

Discerning of spirits

The ability to know for sure if certain behaviors are human or Satanic.

Power

4. Work of Miracles

5. gift of healing

6. Faith

performing miracles

The ability given by God to be able to perform powerful acts, which areperceived by observers
to alter the natural course of events.

Gift of healing

supernatural ability given to the members of the Body of Christ for cure diseases and restore health, apart from the use of natural means.

Faith

An extraordinary ability to know with confidence and confidence and will God's purpose for his work.

Vocal

7. Tongues

8. Interpretation of Tongues

9. Prophecy

Tongues

To speak with God in a language of a person has never learned or to receive and communicate an immediate message from God in a language that a person has never learned.

Interpretation of Tongues

The ability to understand and make known in a colloquial language the message of a person who speaks in tongues.

Prophecy

The special ability to receive and communicate an immediate message of God to his people through a divinely anointed and inspired expression.

Spiritual gifts:

1 Corinthians 12: 8-10

Fruits of the Holy Spirit

Galatians 5: 22-23

*joy

*love

*peace

*Patience

*Goodness

*Faith

*Meekness

*Temperance

Agape love: divine love, a strong fire, tender, compassionate, devotion to the well-being of a person joy

Chara: Emotional excitement, joy, joy for the blessings received or for oneself and others

Gifts of the ministry

*Apostles

*Prophets

*Evangelists

*Pastors

*Teachers

Apostle

• God appointed ambassadors given authority to establish the founding government in a certain area. An apostle listens to the Holy Spirit and puts things in order, according to the health, growth, maturity and dissemination of the Church.

• Establish, strengthen, Reform

• Luke 6: 12-16, 1 Corinthians 12: 28-29

Prophet

• Moved by the Holy Spirit, has the power to instruct, console, encourage, reprimand, exhort with condemning the listeners.

• 5 Major and minor 12

• Intercession, edification, exhortation, Comfort

• 1 Corinthians 14: 1-5, Ezekiel 3: 17-21, Ezekiel 33: 1-16 and 33, Deuteronomy 18: 20-22

Evangelist

• supernatural ability to share the Gospel to unbelievers in such a way as to make them become disciples and responsible members of the Body of Christ.

• Phillip; Acts 21: 8, Timothy; 2 Timothy 4: 5

Pastors

• The ability given to assume a long-term responsibility for the welfare of a body of believers.

• Jeremiah 3:15, John 10: 12-14

Teachers

• The ability to communicate information, relevant to the Body of Christ in a way that allows others to learn. To make clear the biblical truth in such a way that the listeners can teach the information to others.

• 1 Timothy 2: 7, 2 Timothy 1:11, Acts 13: 1

Purpose of the gifts

1. Perfecting of the Saints

2. For the work of the ministry

3. For the building up of the Body of Christ

4. Until we all reach the unity of faith

5. of the knowledge of the Son of God

6. unite a perfect man

7. to the measure of the stature of the fullness of Christ

8. That we are not children, shaken from here to there, and took every wind of doctrine, by light of men, and cunning, by which lurk to deceive.

9. But following the truth in love can grow in Him in all things, which is the head, that is, Christ.

10. Of whom the whole body is composed and well connected to each other and compacted by all the joints that, according to the effective operation in the measure of each member, receives its growth in the Body for the building of this in love

*1 Peter 4:11

Speaking - Service

• Work of the Holy Spirit

• John 14: 16-17, 26

Christology "The Study of Christ"

The main concerns of the Doctrine of Christ

• virgin birth

• impeccability

• Co-equality with the Father

• vicarious death

• The burial

• resurrection

• Isaiah 7: 13-15

Virgin birth

*Isaiah 7: 13-15

*Matthew 1: 18-25.

*Luke 1: 26-36

*Hebrews 4:15

*2 Corinthians 5:21

Co-equal with the Father

*John 1: 1.

*John 10:30

*John 14: 7-9

*Romans 3:25 25

*1 John 2: 2

*1 John 4:10

Baptized burial: baptism; usually; immersion in water, symbolizing purification or regeneration and admission to Christ, submerge the introduction or placement of a thing in a new environment or in conjunction with another person in order to alter its condition or its previous environment or condition.

It refers to the act of God introducing a sinner who believes in a vital union with Jesus Christ, so that the believer may have the power of his broken sin nature and the divine nature implanted through his identification with Christ in his death, burial and resurrection, bringing the theme of the Kingdom of God.

Resurrection

*1 Peter 1: 3-4

* 1 Peter 3:21 21

*Philippians 3:10 10

Intercession

* Hebrews 7: 24-25

*Juan 17

God created the human race to love and serve him and to enjoy a relationship with him.

Theological meaning of human creation (Principles)

The fact that human beings were created means that there is no independent existence (we have not created ourselves).

We will not live forever (we have an initial and final date).

Man lives in time. God lives in eternity.

Questions to ask:

Do things in our life contribute to the glory of God and the fulfillment of his plan?

Our work, education, everything we do; How do they fall in line with what God has told us to do?

1. Humanity is a part of creation. As part of everything else that was created, we have been created with that as well.

2. Human beings have a unique place in creation. Everything else that was created was created according to its kind. With us, we are created in his image and take dominion and authority over everything else.

3. There is a common bond between all human beings.

4. There are definite limitations on humanity. We will all face death.

5. Our limitations are not inherently bad.

6. Humans are something wonderful. We are very well, because God created us in his own image. We are fearful and wonderfully. We are special for God. We have hope!

Views of the image of God and how it should be portrayed

God's point of view is determined by something within us. When we see the image of God it is composed of various characteristics and gifts that are within us.

(Psychological / Spiritual, Love, Strength, Wisdom, Understanding) Internal characteristics / relational qualities based on the relationship we have with God, spiritually, or how we relate to each other.

Functional Based on duty or position We fill in the world (ie, functions / talents: Musician, teacher, preacher, pastor, who rules over people, etc. It is not something that they were created to do that can only be done.

Angelology The study of the angels

The divisions of the Angels

*Demonic

The purpose of the Angels

Angels as messengers

*Daniel 8: 15-16

*Luke 1: 11-19

*Matthew 1: 18-21

*Luke 2: 12-20

*Mark 16: 5-7

*Luke 24: 4-7

Angels as guardians

*Psalm 91:11

*Psalm 34: 7

*Hebrews 1-14

*Matthew 4:11

*Daniel 6:22

Angels as warriors

*Revelations 12: 7-9

*Daniel 10:13

*Daniel 12: 1

*2 Kings 19:35

*Isaiah 37:36

Angels as Worshipers

*Revelation 7:11

Angels are not to be worshiped

*Colossians 2:18

Hamartiology "Doctrine of Sin"

Biblical perspectives

1. Sin is an inclination towards the inside

2. Sin is rebellion and disobedience

3. Without implying spiritual incapacity

4. Sin is incomplete fulfillment of God's standards

The definitions of transgression:

1. an act that goes against a law, rule, or code of conduct; an offense. Ps.51: 1,

2. wickedness: an intrinsically evil act Luke 15:12

3. Error: a deviation from the right Ps 51: 9, Romans 3:23

4. does not comply with the divine norm.

5. transgression: the intrusion of one's will into the sphere of divine authority. Ephesians 2:1

6. Illegality: spiritual anarchy 1 Tim 1: 9

7. Unbelief: an insult to divine veracity John 16: 9

Source of sin

1. The desire to enjoy things

2. The desire to get things

3. The desire to do things - 1 John 2:16

Sin and our relationship with God

1. divine disapproval

2. The fault

3. The death penalty

4. Physical death

5. Spiritual death

6. Eternal Death

Sin and the sinner

1. Slavery escape from reality

2. The denial of sin

3. self-deception

4. Insensitivity

5. egocentrism

6. Restlessness

Sin affects with Others

1. Competition

2. The inability to empathize

3. The rejection of the authority

4. The inability to love

Soteriology "The study of salvation"

1. The conversion

2. Substitution

3. Reconciliation

4. propiciación

5. Referral

6. Redemption

7. Regeneration

8. The imputation

9. Approval

10. Supplication

11. Justification

12. Sanctification

13. The glorification

14. Preservation

To effect salvation with success; the complete delivery of someone or something of an imminent danger. To be freed from the penalty, power and presence of sin.

Hebrews 9: 24-28

Salvation- Salvation is a process that consists of three parts.

• Justification

• Sanctification

• Glorification

Justification

Justification is an act, not a process. Romans 5: 1

• There are no degrees of justification; every believer has the same correct position before God. Romans 3:22.

Justification does not mean that God makes us righteous Romans 8:33; but in that he declares us righteous. Romans 3:24

Justification is a legal matter; God puts the righteousness of Christ on our account in the place of our sin and no one can or will change this account. Romans 4: 3. Romans 4:25 Corinthians 5:21 Galatians 3: 27-28 27

• Justification is received by faith. Romans 3:24: Galatians 3:11

• Justification means declaring righteous and treating as such. Romans 4: 4, 5

• Never changes. When the sinner trusts Christ; God declares you righteous, and that the declaration will not be repealed. God sees in us and treats us as if we had never sinned.

Imputation a charge or claim that someone has done something undesirable; an accusation.

3 Types of imputation

1. The imputation of Adam's sin to the human race.

2. The imputation of the sin of the Race in Christ

3. The imputation of God's justice Through the propitiatory sacrifice of Christ in the believing sinner.

1. **The imputation of Adam's sin to the human race**

*Romans 5: 12,19

*Romans 3:23

*1 Corinthians 15:22

2. **The imputation of the sin of the race in Jesus Christ.**

*Isaiah 53: 5

*Hebrews 2: 9

*1 Peter 2:24

*2 Corinthians 5:21

3. **The imputation of God's justice Through the propitiatory sacrifice of Christ in the believing sinner.**

*Romans 3:21

*Philippians 3: 9

• Sanctification is both positional and practical.

*1 Corinthians 1:30

*Romans 6-8

What salvation?

• It is not the eradication of the sinful nature

*Philippians 3: 12-14

*James 3: 2

*1 John 1: 8

*1 John 2: 1-6

What it is?

Sanctification is found in some form in the Old Testament and 300 times in the New Testament 760 times for a total of 1,060 and the basic meaning in all cases is "set apart".

• God sanctifies people, places and things. Exodus 19:10 Leviticus 27:14.

What is God's will for us?

• Once we are justified or declared just God begins a work in us to make us righteous, God does not intend to leave us in our condition.

*Philippians 1: 6

*1 Peter 1: 15 - 16

*1 Thessalonians 4: 1-3

*Ephesians 5: 25-27

*Romans 12: 1

• In Romans chapter 6 God puts out the plan for us in relation to the whole life process of growing in grace and spiritual maturity, which is sanctification. This plan consists of 4 simple orders and are labeled attitudes of sanctification.

Sanctification attitudes

We are to know: Romans 6: 1-10

We have recognition: To count as true; Romans 6: 11-12

1. We are to perform: Romans 6: 16-23

2. We must serve: Romans 6: 18-23

Prophetic training

Prophets

1. Those with the gift of prophecy

2. Those who operate with the spirit of prophecy

Types of prophetic impressions (flows)

Nataf: This means "drop like the rain". It comes to us little by little and accumulates in our buckets over a period of time.

Massa: This is used to refer to the "hand of the Lord" that frees the "burden of the Lord". When the hand of God comes upon us, it imparts something to us. When his hand rises, his load remains.

Nabiy: This word refers to the action of "flow forward". It also carries with it the thought of "bubbling like a fountain, dropping, rising, spilling and sprouting."

Prophetic protocol

1. Always prophecy in love. 1Corinthians 14: 1

2. Prophecy according to your level of faith. Romans 12: 6

3. Avoid being too demonstrative, dramatic, theatrical or colorful when ministering prophetically. Excessive movements of the hand Excessive speaking in tongues

4. Use wisdom when you minister to someone of the opposite sex. Place your hands on their shoulders or have someone of the same sex to place their hands for healing or impartation.

5. Do not allow people to worship you. Be humble and remember to worship Jesus.

6. Do not be a "lone Ranger". Learn to minister with others. We know in part and we prophesy in part.

7. Never contradict the Scriptures. Prophets and prophetic persons must be students of the word.

8. Know your strengths and limitations. Everyone has their strengths and limitations. Knowing yours could be the difference between success and failure. It is not a competition We are not trying to outdo others

9. Remember that the spirit of the prophet is subject to the prophets. No prophet has all the revelation and it is important for prophetic persons to work together to fulfill the assignment of heaven to earth. 1 Corinthians 14:32

10. Do not be repetitive. Once you have thrown the word, it is not necessary to repeat the same continuously to convey the message. Learn to stop when the Holy Spirit stops.

11. Speak in the first person. You are the voice of the Lord on earth. You are speaking what the Holy Spirit wants you to say.

Spiritual warfare training

Learn how to recognize, discern and defeat the spiritual forces that oppose the Kingdom of God through Spiritual Warfare

Spiritual warfare: the plan of the enemy

* Causes us to abort our destiny

* Because we disobey God

* Because we are committed

* Make us lose the mark, be in divine disagreement

* Causes us to be tormented, bound, frustrated stagnant, sterile (unsuccessful), double minded and unstable,

Spiritual warfare: enemy tactics

* Disappointment

* Distraction

* Depression

* Discouragement

* Division

Spiritual warfare: our enemy

I do not believe that everything isn't the devil and, therefore, we must take responsibility for our actions and renew our mind and crucify our flesh. By doing this, we will see that many of our problems will be addressed. Then we can see clearly to deal with the devil and his demonic forces.

* The Mind (without renewing)

* The Flesh (without criticism)

* The devil

* Demonic forces

Our Enemy: The Mind

Although we have a real enemy in the form of the devil and his cohorts, it is of the greatest importance for believers to renew their minds. Many times, the biggest battle a believer will face will be in his mind. If we can condition our mind to be strong and focused and to understand the purpose, then we will begin to walk in the fullness of discipline and order as we fulfill the mandate of heaven for our lives.

*Romans 12: 2

*2 Corinthians 10: 5

2 Corinthians tells us that we must reject imaginations and everything that is exalted against the knowledge of God in our lives. This is not a casual action but a violent one. We literally have to order violently and do what is necessary for us to reject it. I often give the analogy that a thought is literally in our head and we have to grab it and hit it on the ground as fast and strong as possible. This is how the believer should operate when it comes to dealing with the thoughts that have captivated our mind.

Our Enemy: The Flesh

The next enemy that the believer must deal with is the flesh. Many times, we blame the devil for things that are really the works of our flesh.

* Romans 7:18

* James 1: 13-14

* Galatians 5: 19-21

Once we have dealt with our mind and our flesh accurately, we can see clearly what the devil really is. Too many believers continue to go to the altar to pray for things that they have the ability to control if they only apply prayer, meditation on the word, discipline, responsibility and obedience.

Our enemy: the devil

* 1 Peter 5: 8

* John 10:10

The last enemy in the area of spiritual warfare is the demonic forces that come to frustrate us, harass us and antagonize us. We must realize that if Jesus and other biblical characters deal with demonic forces we will also do so.

When Satan rebelled, he took 1/3 of the angels with him and they are the forces that work demonically to keep us from obeying God and fulfilling the mandate of Heaven for our lives. Learning to discern them and how they work is imperative for success in the life of the believer. If we do not learn to discern, eventually we will be defeated by what we did not know was there.

Our Enemy: Demonic Forces

* Ephesians 6:12

* Principalities: archangel rule, magisterium of angels and demons

* **Exousia:** the power to choose, of authority, of rule or government

* The rulers of the darkness of this world:

* **Kosmokrator**: Lord of the world prince of this era the devil and his demons

* **Skotos**: of dark sight or blindness

Demonic forces: Indicators

* 1. Chronic marital problems

* 2. Chronic disease

* 3. Mental illness

* 4. Chronic financial problems

* 5. Repeated miscarriages

* 6. Being prone to accidents

Authority of the Believer

* Luke 10:19

Common doors

* Sin (disobedience)

* Emotional wounds

* Generation curses

* Bitterness and lack of forgiveness

* Contracts and agreements

* Placement of hands

Spiritual warfare: the door of sin

* Sins of omission: not doing something good or right when you know you should do it.

* Sins of commission: knowing that something is wrong and doing it anyway

* Sexual: Pornography, Homosexuality, Lesbianism, Fornication, Adultery, Masturbation, Fetishes

* Crime: murder, robbery, rape

Spiritual warfare: the door of emotional damage

* Childhood

* Trauma

* Demons like to stay within certain families Check family history

* Spoken word curses Spiritual warfare: bitterness and lack of forgiveness

* Matthew 18: 21-22, 34-35

* James 3: 14-15

* Hebrews 12:15

Spiritual warfare: contracts and agreements

Examples: Festivals, Rituals, Artifacts, Occultism, Secret Societies, Nature; Water, fire, sun, stars, moon

Spiritual warfare - Divination

* Divination / prediction

* Knowledge that comes from the demons

* Psychics

* Ouiji Boards

* Charismatic divination

Spiritual warfare - witchcraft

* Tools

* Potions

* Charms

* Magic

* Spells and hexes

* Drugs that alter the mind

Spiritual warfare - Imposition of hands

* Method of transfer or delivery

* Made in prayer

* Not done indiscriminately

* 1 Timothy 5:22

Spiritual warfare: our motive

We often hear that those who operate in the ministry of liberation are petty and unpleasant and lack the love of Christ. We must always understand that we must operate in the love of Christ for those we minister to and that our main motive should always be love and compassion. Our hearts should be the same as God's for his people and we would like to see them free from all that keeps them captive. No one wants to be held captive, even if they have begun to enjoy what holds them captive. Many times, this can happen and will happen in which a believer will have been obligated for so long that they will really think they are called to enjoy bondage /strongholds or that this is what they are. This is the lie of the enemy. Jesus came to liberate the captive and as we are called to his side and we have passed the baton, we must now defend the cause of Christ on earth to free the captive, just as Paul instructed Timothy "When they oppose themselves"

* Isaiah 61: 1-3

* Luke 7: 13-14, 10:33, 15:20

* Matthew 9:36, 14: 13-21, 15:32, 18:27, 20:34

* Mark 1:41, 6:34, 8: 2, 9:22

Spiritual warfare: our authority

* Luke 10:19

* John 14: 12-14

* Mark 16: 15-18

Spiritual warfare: common forces operating in the church

* **Jezebel**: challenges authority

* **Absalom**: rebellion against spiritual fathers and mothers

* **Korah / Miriam**: challenges authority

* Python: challenged apostle Paul

* Leviathan: PRIDE

These certainly are not all, but this gives a brief description of what you can find in the church in regards to spiritual warfare.

Spiritual warfare: Groupings

Addiction - Bitterness

Leviathan - Accusation

Absalom - Passivity

Jealousy - Rejection

Lust - insecurity

Religious - Conflict

Jezebel - Ahab

Infirmity - Mind binding

Judas, Sanballat, Tobias

Contentious - Fatigue

Corruption - Concern

Challenging - Perfection

Appollyon - Impatience

Jebusite - Pride - Cults

Squid - false charges

Python – Religious

Heritage - Cursing

Heaviness - Spiritism

Laziness - Fears

Molech - Gluttony

Fear - Competition

Doubt – Persecution

Spiritual war: Ministerial healing

1. Healing through the laying on of hands

2. Healing through liberation

3. Healing through breaking curses

4. Healing through anointing oil

5. Healing through faith

6. Healing by virtue or touch

7. Healing through the presence of God

8. Healing through prayer

9. Healing through the gift of healing

10. Healing through fasting

11. Healing through the word

Finally, once you have begun to understand the liberation and what forces are operating, it is necessary to know how to help people to free themselves from the forces that have bound them.

Intercessory prayer training

* Learn to participate and emerge victorious in intercessory prayer

Prophetic intercession

* Call intercessors, characteristics, authority and lifestyle

* The importance and value of the intercessor

* Types of intercessors

* Prophetic words of war

* Prophetic activations of the intercessor

Definition of Intercession

* "Intercession can be defined as a holy and believing prayer through which someone pleads with God on behalf of another person or others who desperately need God's intervention."

Purpose of the intercession

Intimate prayer with the Lord will give you the strength to overcome the attacks of the enemy.

A powerful weapon will have the living word with the manifestation of the holy spirit intimidated in prayer will take you to other spiritual levels. You will receive instructions for your assignation. The purpose of the intercessor in the local church is to ensure that all areas of the church are continuously covered.

* Avoid the trial

* Safe healing

* Ensure the release

* Get restoration

* Encourage repentance

* Approach God as Abba Father

Intercessors Authority

* Intercession gives us authority to oversee and cover our ministry, ministerial leaders, nations, kings, all areas of government, family members, ministerial partners, as well as the Body of Christ.

Two Hebrew words for intercession

1 **Paga**: find, plead, intercede, fall (for hostility), hit, touch (as limit) to light, interpose, attack, reach the mark, push, rush someone with hostile violence, or kill

2.**Tephilla**: To intercede and sing your prayers and intercessions to God in formal worship.

* Hebrews 13:15

Obstacles to pray

Doubt: unbelief is probably the biggest obstacle to unanswered prayer. (Mark 11: 21-23, James 1: 6-8)

Pride / Own: God hates pride! Pride prevents sincere prayer because it avoids humility.

* Romans 12: 3 God is love (Lack of love) We cannot be wrong with man and with God. Neither can we displease who God loves.

* Matthew 5: 44-45

* 1 John 4:20

Refusing to do your part: we cannot be sincere in praying for the ungodly unless we are willing to make some attempt to put them under the influence of the Gospel. You do not have to pray and ask God to do something that you already have the power to do.

Praying only in secret: God honors unified; corporate prayer and "agreed".

* Matthew 18: 19-20

Lack of forgiveness: you cannot enter into prayer with bitterness and forgiveness and expect to leave with blessings. The lack of forgiveness is an essential ingredient for answered prayer.

* Mark 11: 25

* Matthew 6: 14-15

Wrong reasons: when our motives are not correct, our prayers will not have power. Your prayers should not benefit you alone, but should benefit the Kingdom of God.

* James 4: 3

Idols in your life: when you look at your life regarding your career, your possessions and your family, are you willing to renounce them for God? If not, they have become idols in your life. When we eliminate idols, we mature so that God brings revival in our lives.

* Ezekiel 14: 3 Ignore the sovereignty of God: it is important that we follow Christ's example to his disciples in honoring God for what he is.

* Matthew 6: 9-10

Will not delivered: God promises to answer the prayers and grant the requests of those who surrender to him.

* John 15: 7

Sin: If we consider sin in our hearts, God will not listen to us.

* Psalm 66: 18

* Isaiah 59: 1-2

Moses' prayer for the people after the golden calf

*Exodus 32: 11-14

*Exodus 32: 21-34

*Exodus 33:12

The prayer of Solomon in the consecration of the temple

*2 Chronicles 6: 1-42

Work for your children

*Job 1: 5

David's prayer for the liberation of the plague

*1 Chronicles 21:17

Jeremiah's prayer

*Lamentations 2: 20

*Lamentations 5: 1

*Lamentations 5: 9

Paul's prayer for Timothy

*2 Timothy 1: 3

Paul for the Church of Ephesus

*Ephesians 1: 16-19

Prayer for Peter in prison

*Acts 12: 5

*Acts 12: 11-12

Attributes of an intercessor

1. Abandonment

2. Acceptance

3. Responsibility

4. Lawyer

5. Agonizing

6. Armor

Attributes of an intercessor

1. Availability

2. Consciousness

3. Authority Qualities of an intercessor

1. Unconditional love

2. Knowledge of the Word of God

3. Reliability and dedication

4. An educational heart

5. A heart of mercy

6. Honesty and humility

1. Ability to pray positive prayers and blessings

2. A sincere call to prayer

3. Possess the power of reconciliation

4. Possibility of being a team player

5. An adequate understanding of the cross

How to protect the ministry of intercession

1. Protects yourself against fatigue

2. Protect yourself against gossip and murmur

3. Protects yourself against disunity

4. Avoid having your own agenda

5. Keep being humble

6. Always avoid worrying about enemy strategies

The victory comes by through His word His dedication and action.

We have the tools to do the Lord's will remember to apply their daily training in our lives and in times of tribulation pain, sadness.

Keep in communication as these are the moments that the enemy will use to separate from the senor preventing communication. We are not alone because the Lord will never abandon us.

Made in the USA
Columbia, SC
27 August 2024

40686460R00037